BIG-NOTE PIANO

Classical Music's Greatest 1

D0886215

CONTENTS

ISBN 0-634-00373-9

HAL•LEONARD®
CORPORATION
7777 W. BLUEMOUND RD. P.O. BOX 13819 MILWAUKEE, WI 53213

Visit Hal Leonard Online at
www.halleonard.com

AIR ON THE G STRING

By JOHANN SEBASTIAN BACH

Slowly and stately

3

BRIDAL CHORUS
from LOHENGRIN

Music by RICHARD WAGNER

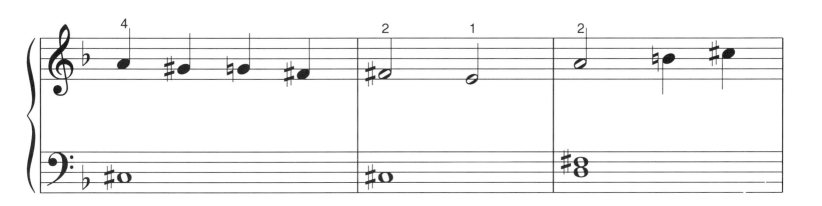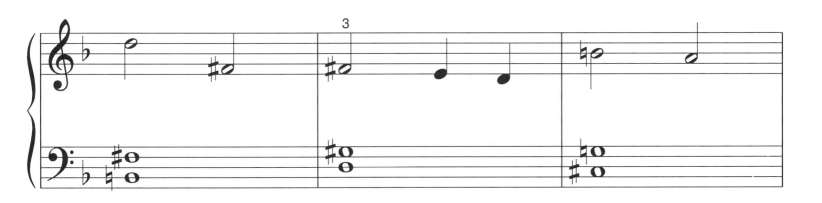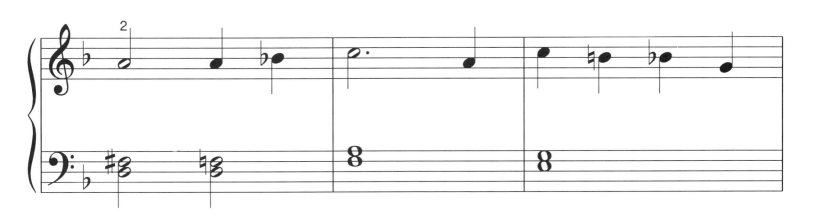

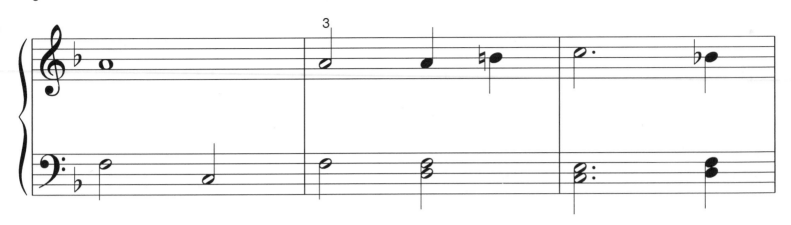

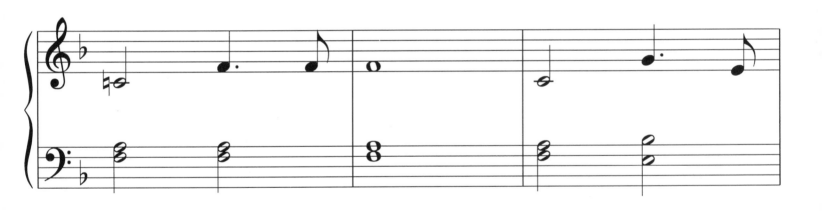

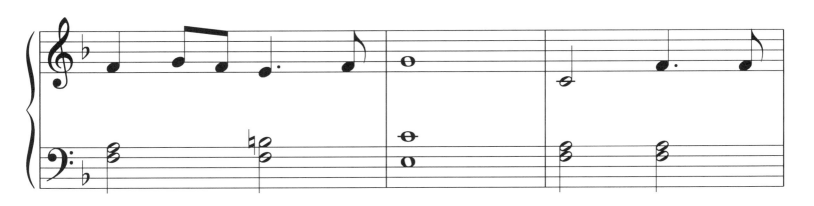

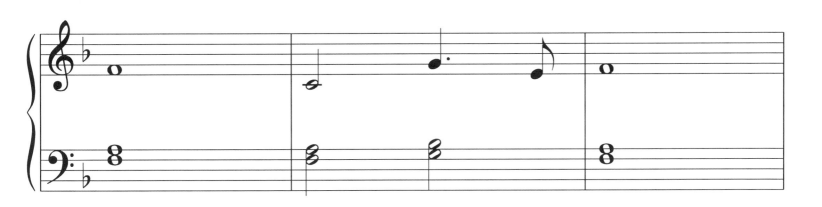

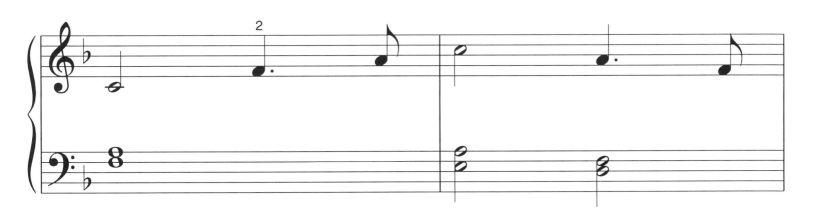

ALLELUIA

By WOLFGANG AMADEUS MOZART

Moderately fast

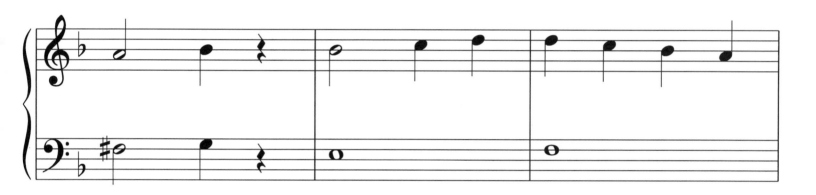

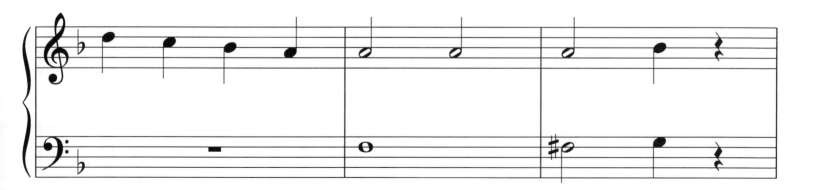

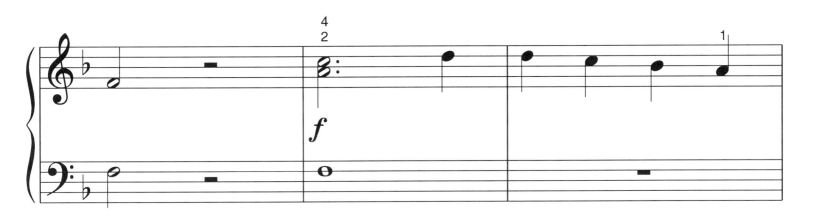

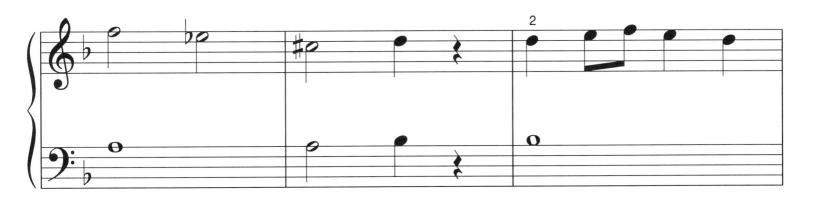

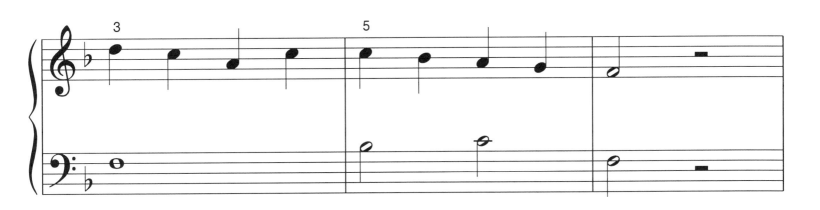

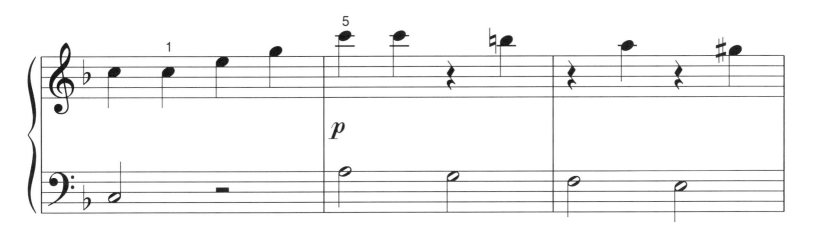

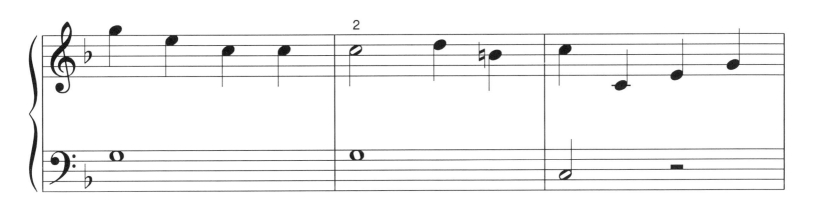

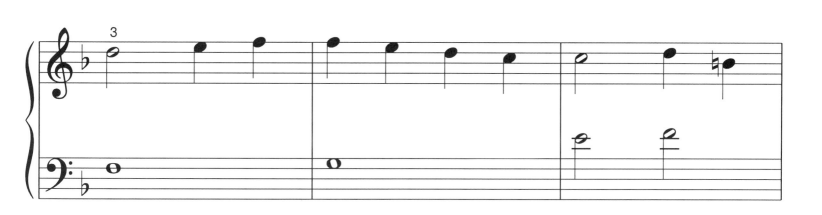

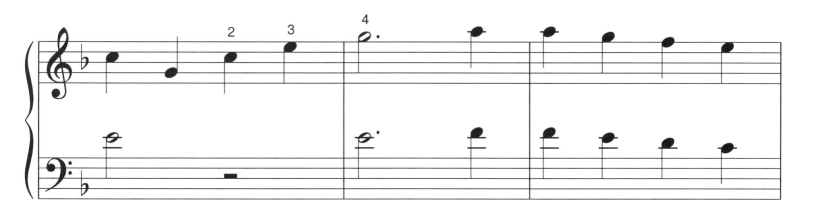

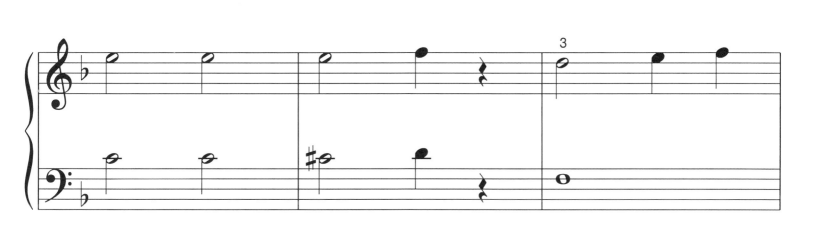

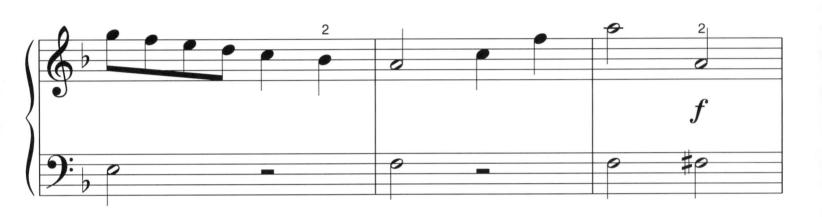

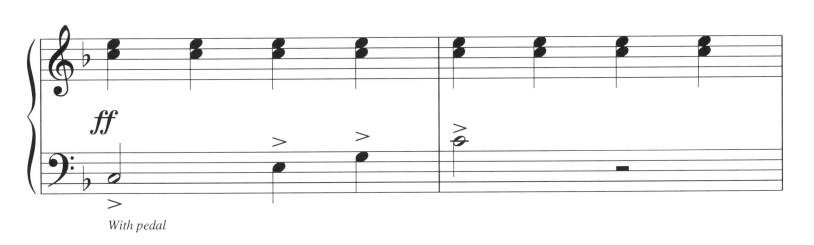

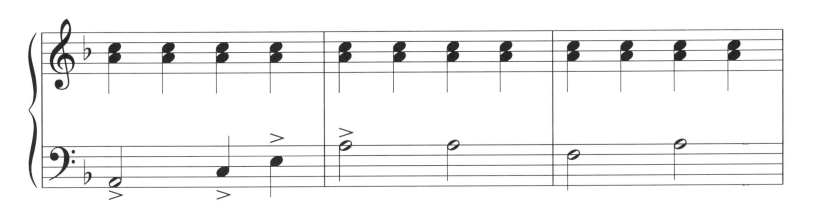

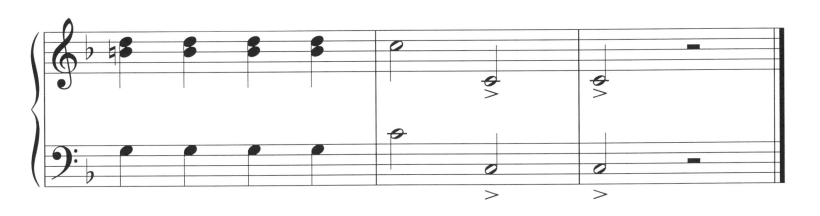

ALSO SPRACH ZARATHUSTRA

By RICHARD STRAUSS

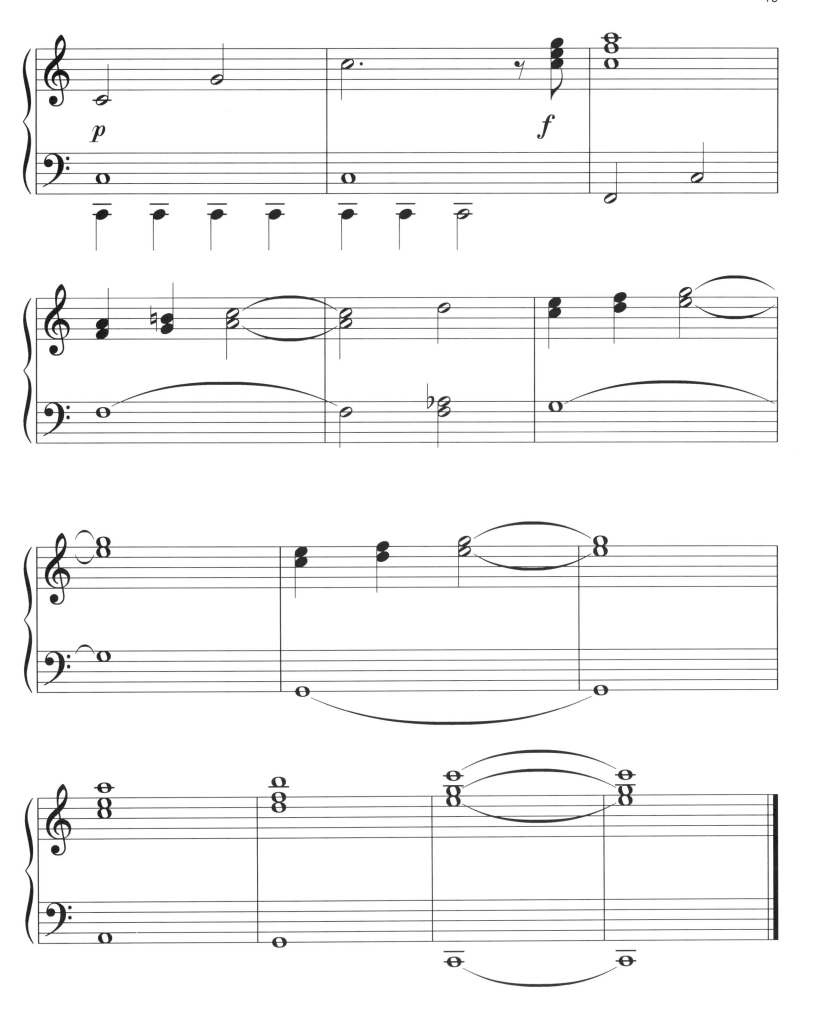

AVE MARIA

By FRANZ SCHUBERT

22

BY THE BEAUTIFUL
BLUE DANUBE

By JOHANN STRAUSS, JR.

Moderately

Fine

D.C. al Fine

CANON IN D

By JOHANN PACHELBEL

29

EINE KLEINE NACHTMUSIK

By WOLFGANG AMADEUS MOZART

Moderately fast

1812 OVERTURE

By PYOTR IL'YICH TCHAIKOVSKY

Moderately fast

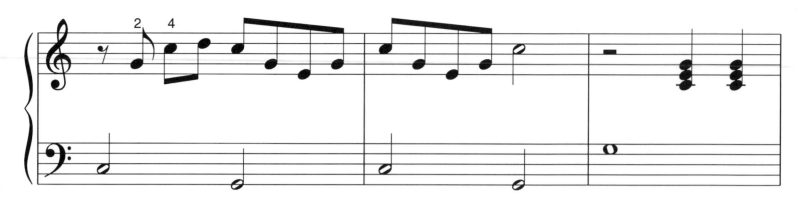

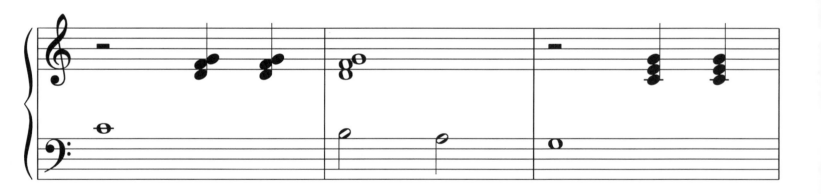

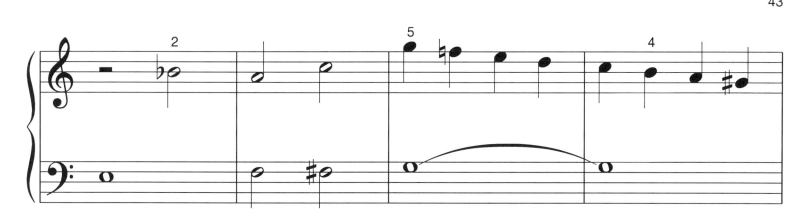

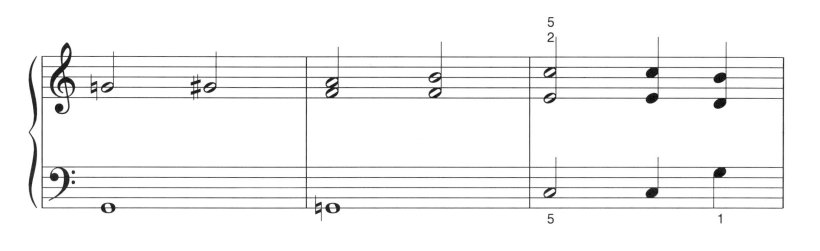

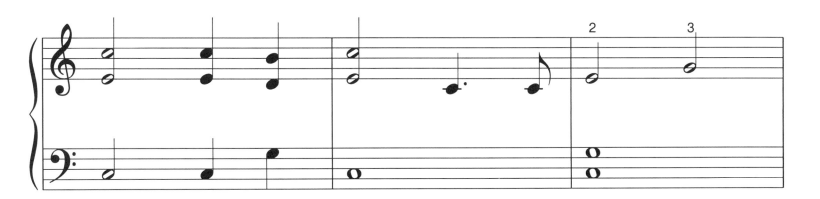

FUNERAL MARCH OF A MARIONETTE

By CHARLES GOUNOD

Moderately fast

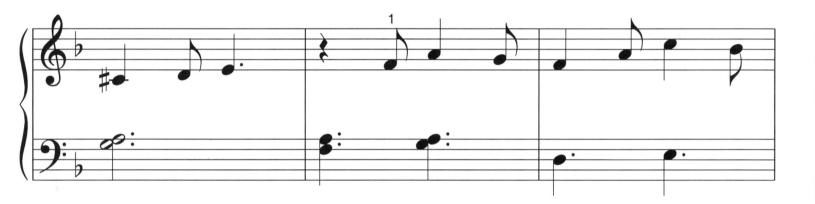

LULLABY
(Cradle Song)

By JOHANNES BRAHMS

Sweetly, with motion

FÜR ELISE

By LUDWIG VAN BEETHOVEN

Gently, moderately slow

49

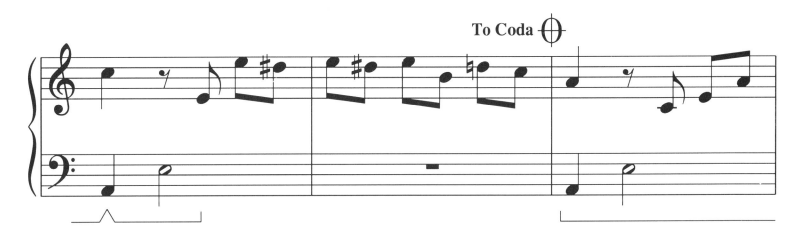

Ped. simile

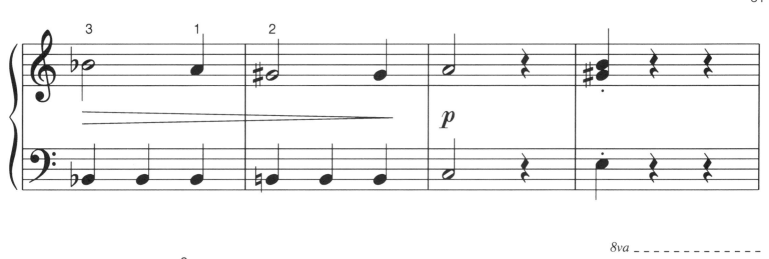

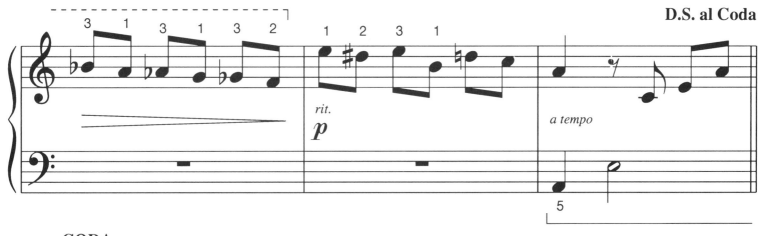

D.S. al Coda

CODA

HALLELUJAH!
from MESSIAH

By GEORGE FRIDERIC HANDEL

IN THE HALL OF
THE MOUNTAIN KING
from PEER GYNT

By EDVARD GRIEG

Like a slow march

MORNING
from PEER GYNT

By EDVARD GRIEG

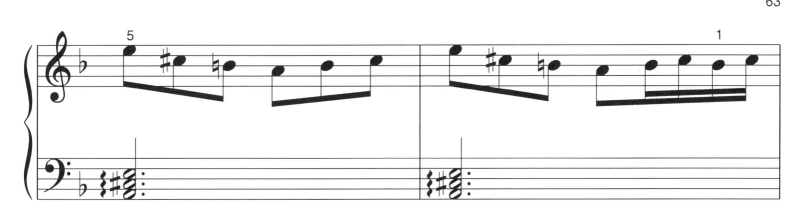

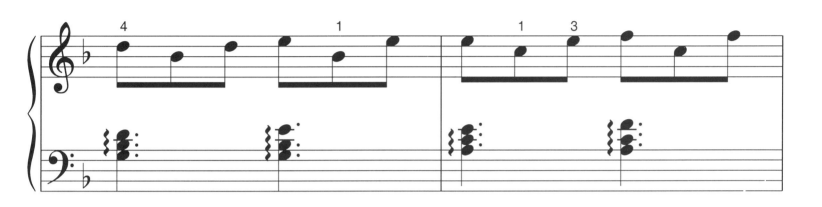

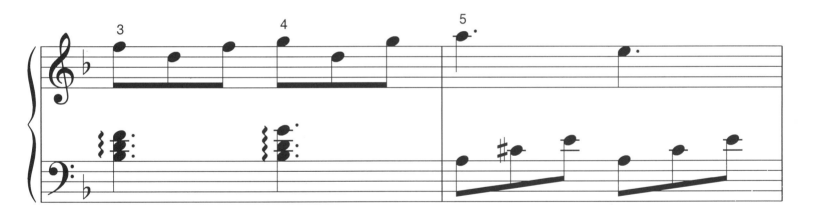

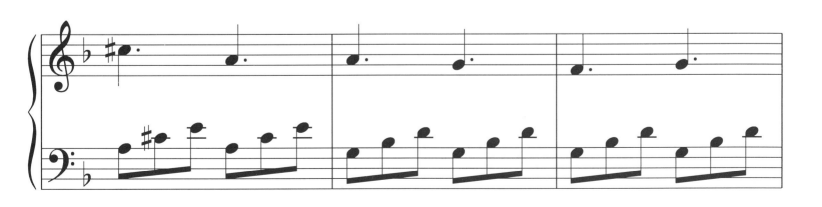

ODE TO JOY

from SYMPHONY NO. 9 IN D MINOR

Words by HENRY VAN DYKE
Music by LUDWIG VAN BEETHOVEN

With spirit

PANIS ANGELICUS
(O Lord Most Holy)

By CÉSAR FRANCK

Slow

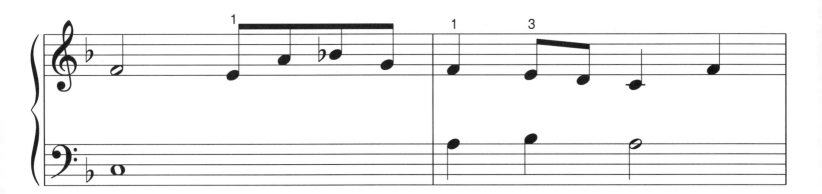

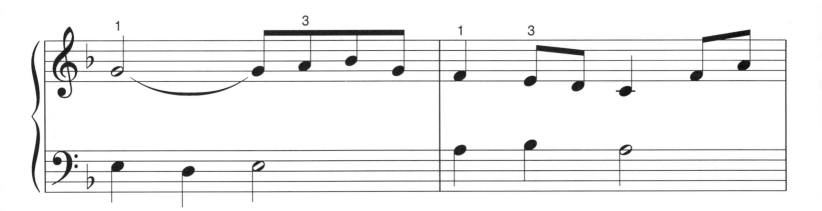

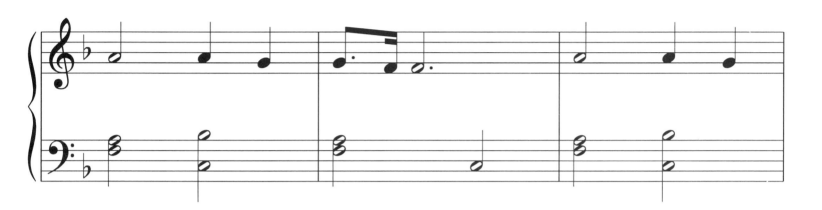

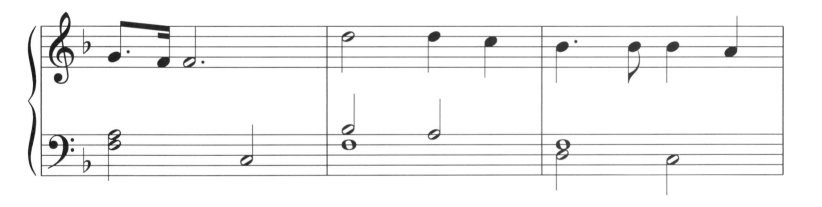

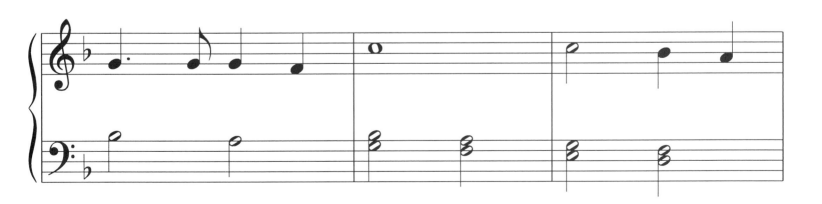

ROMEO AND JULIET
(Love Theme)

By PYOTR IL'YICH TCHAIKOVSKY

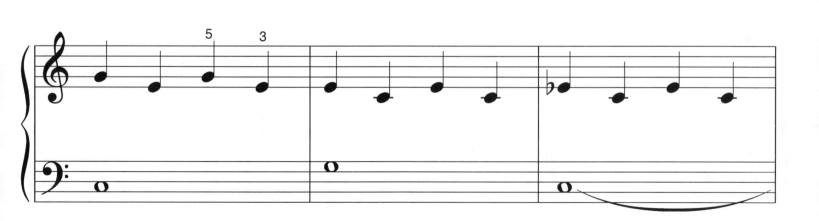

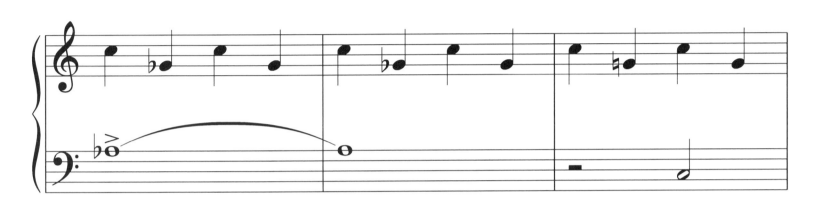

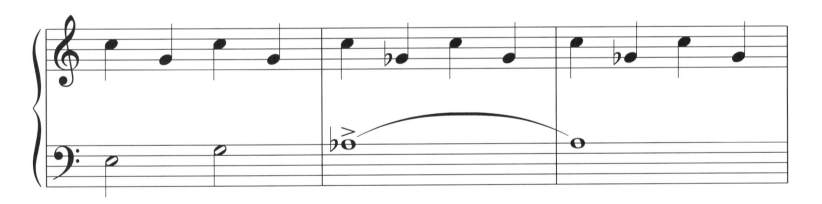

RONDEAU

By JEAN-JOSEPH MOURET

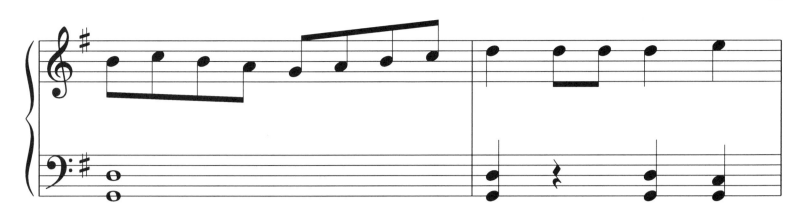

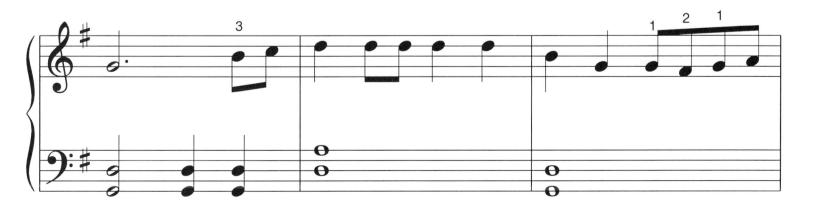

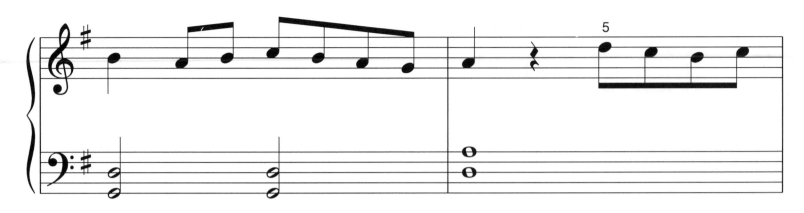

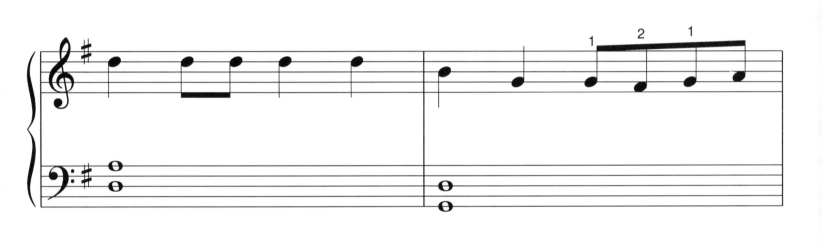

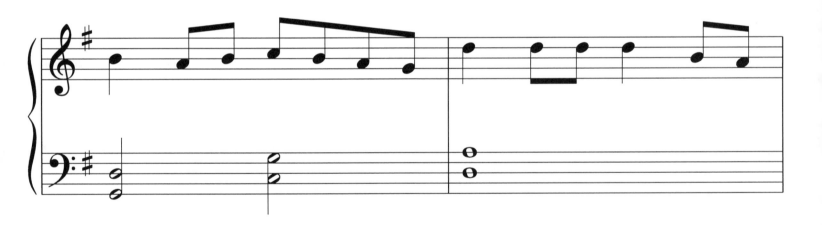

SHEEP MAY SAFELY GRAZE

By JOHANN SEBASTIAN BACH

83

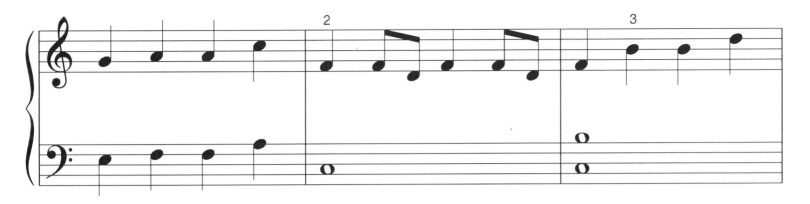

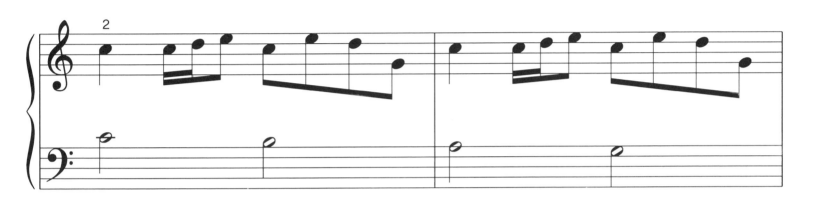

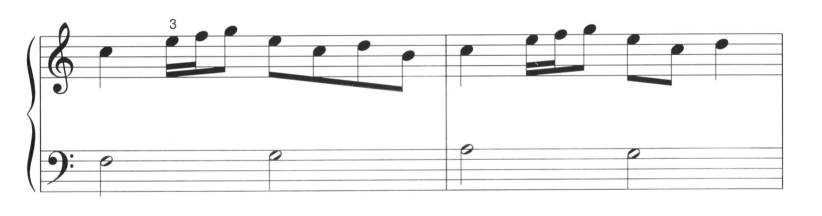

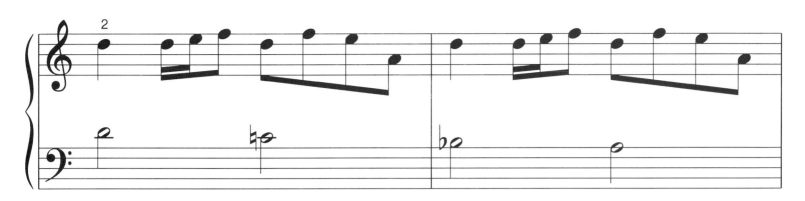

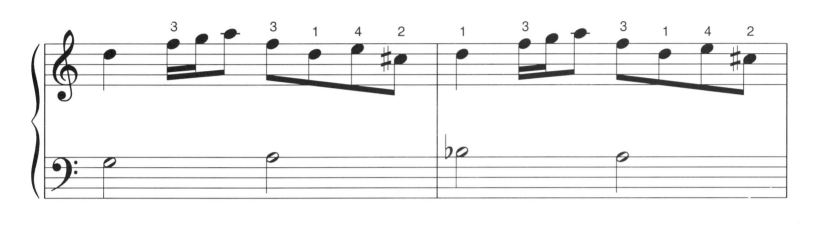

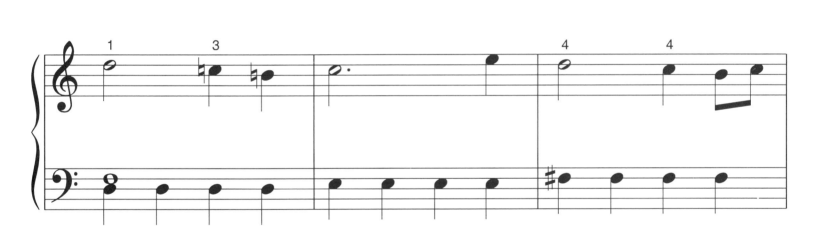

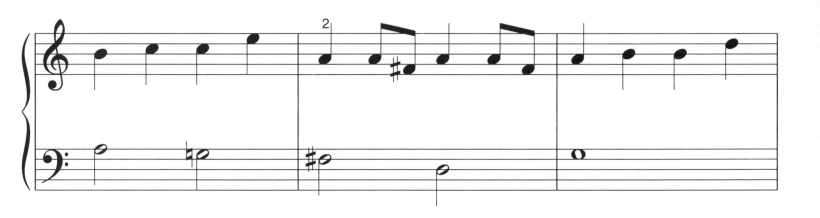

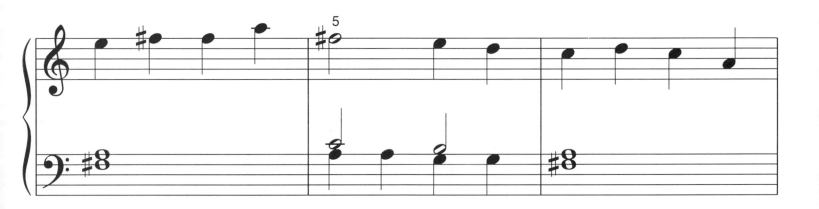

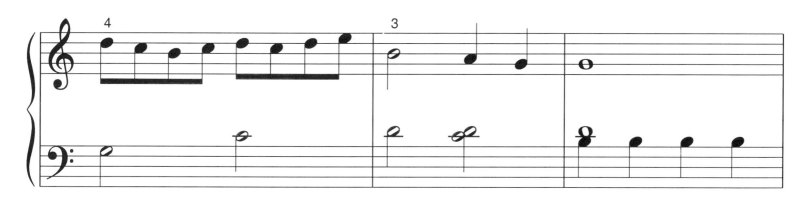

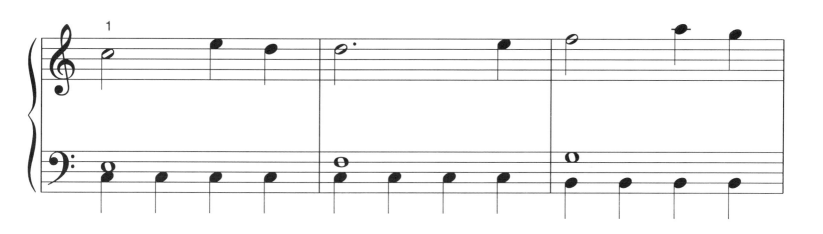

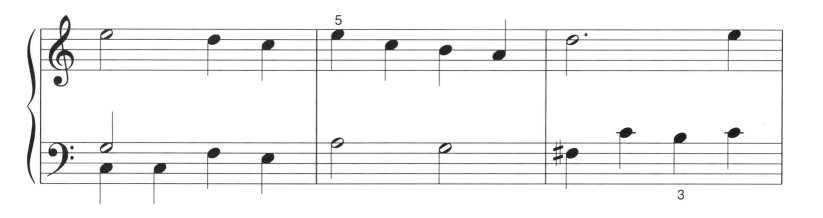

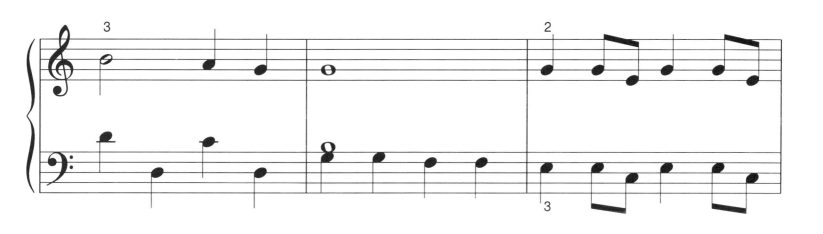

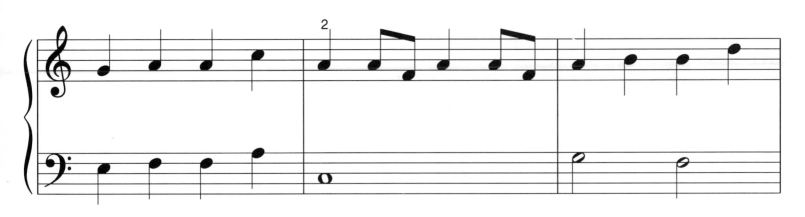

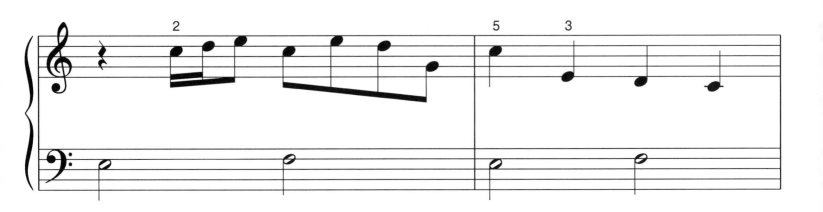

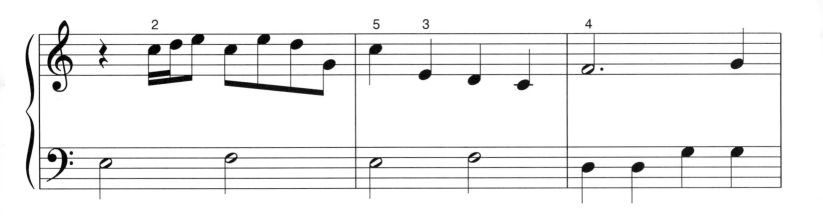

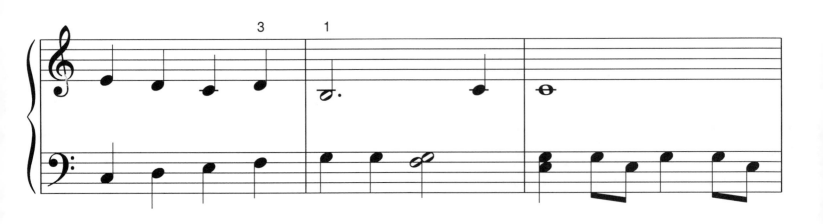

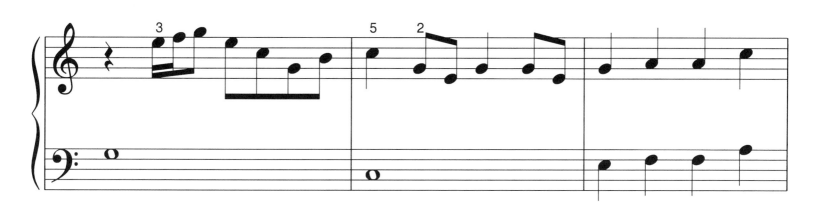

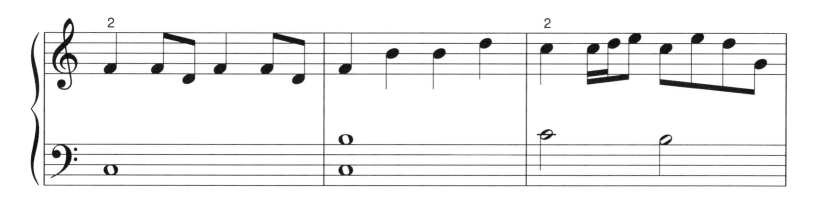

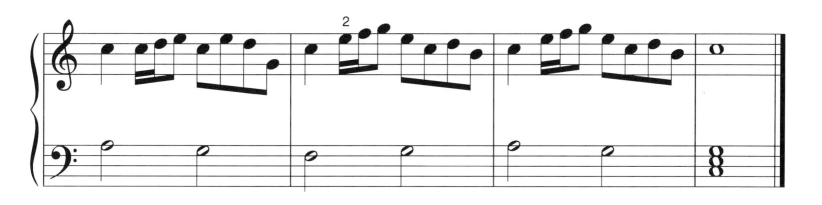

THE SWAN
(Le Cygne)
from CARNIVAL OF THE ANIMALS

By CAMILLE SAINT-SAËNS

Slowly and smoothly

SYMPHONY NO. 9 IN E MINOR

("From The New World"), Second Movement

By ANTONÍN DVORÁK

Slowly

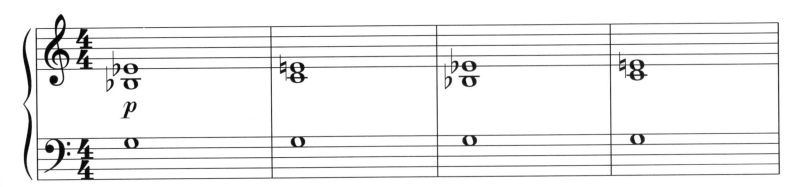

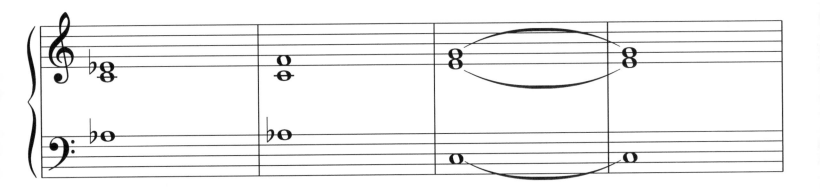

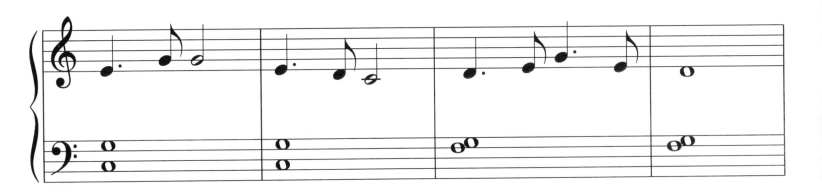

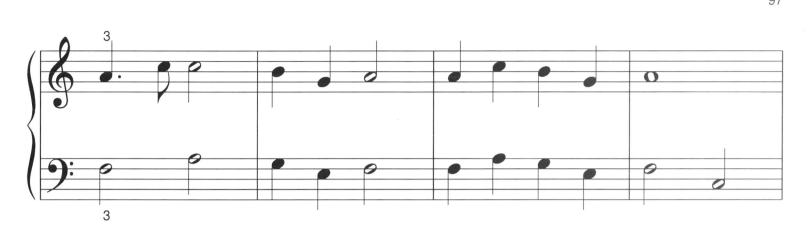

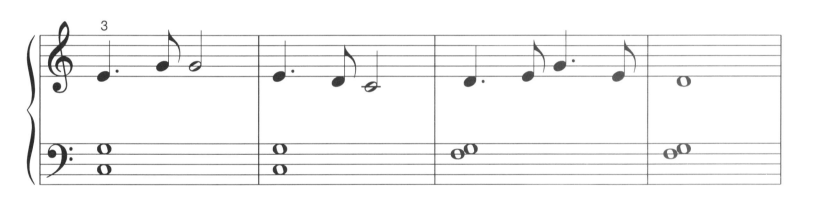

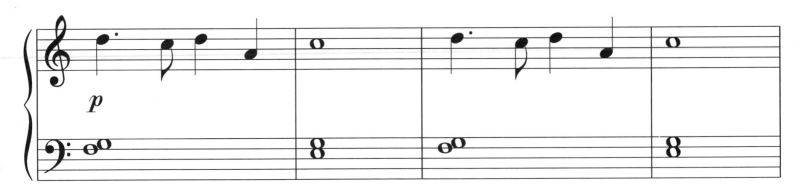

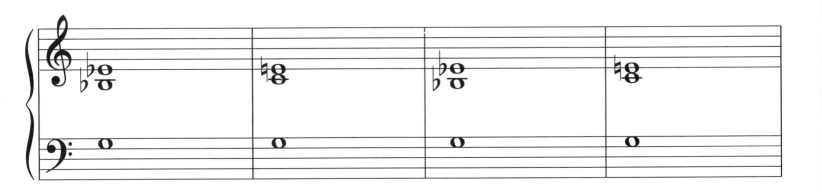

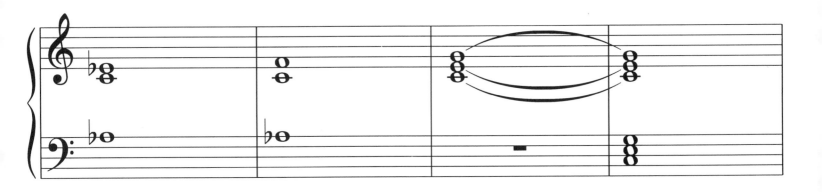

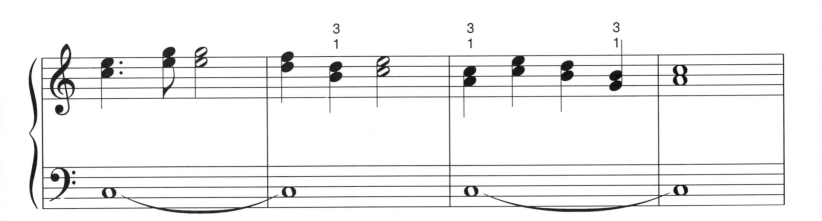

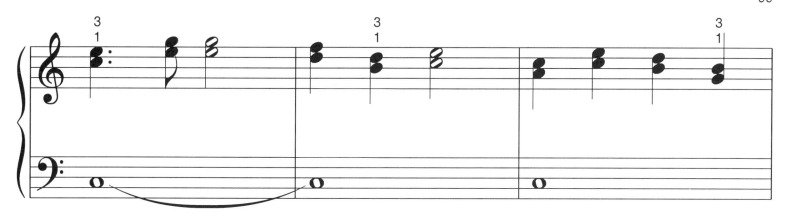

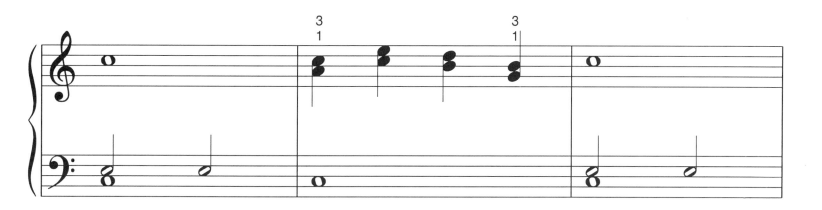

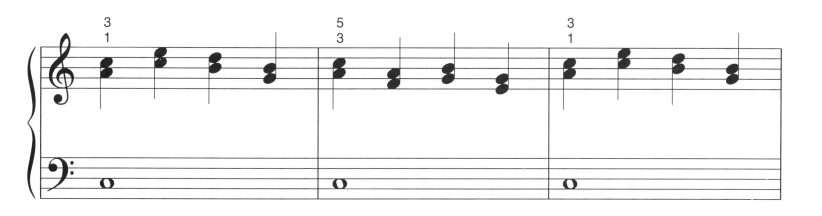

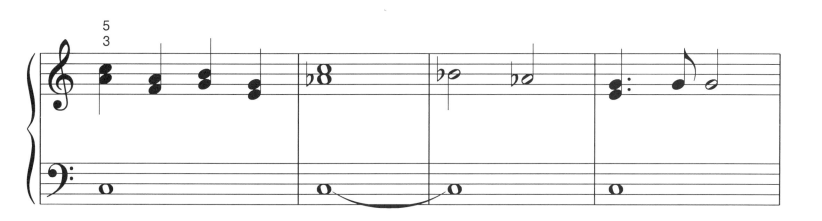

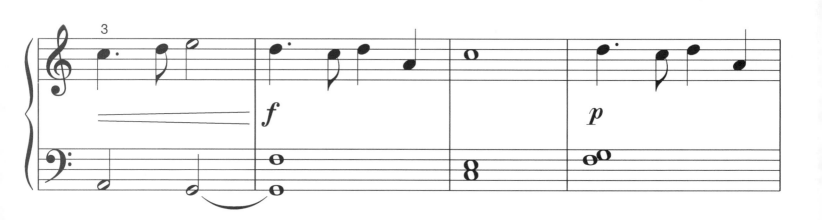

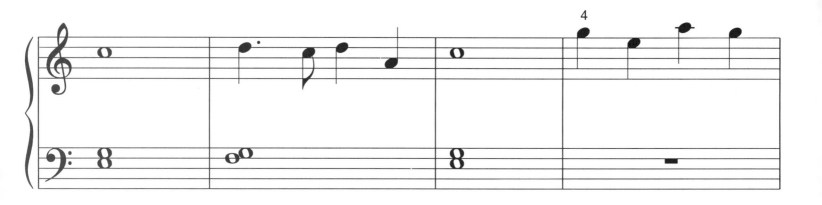

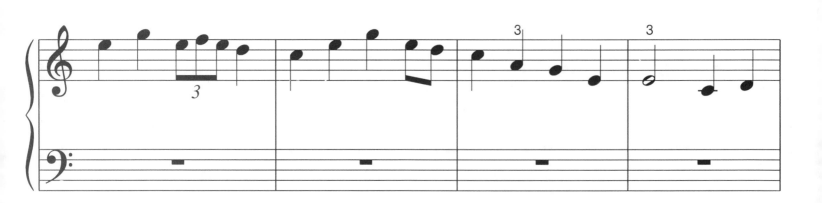

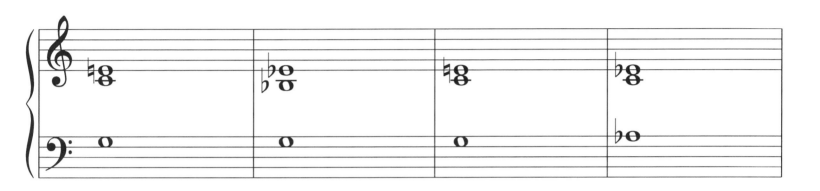

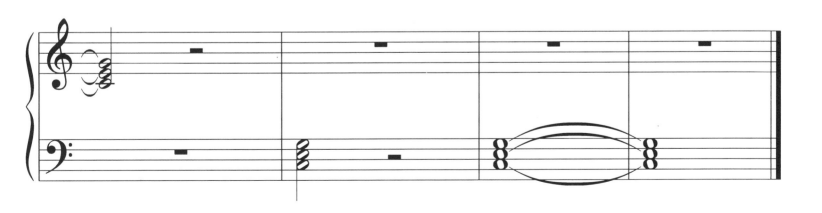

WALTZ OF THE FLOWERS
from THE NUTCRACKER

By PYOTR IL'YICH TCHAIKOVSKY

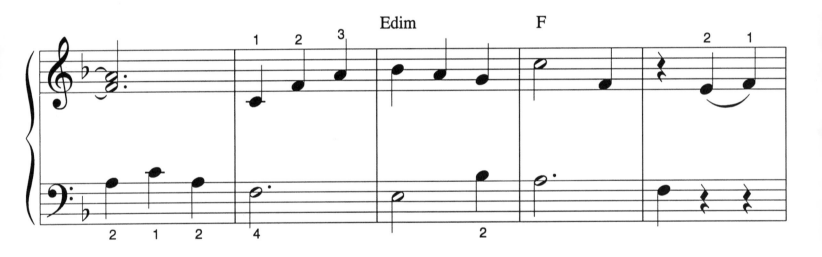

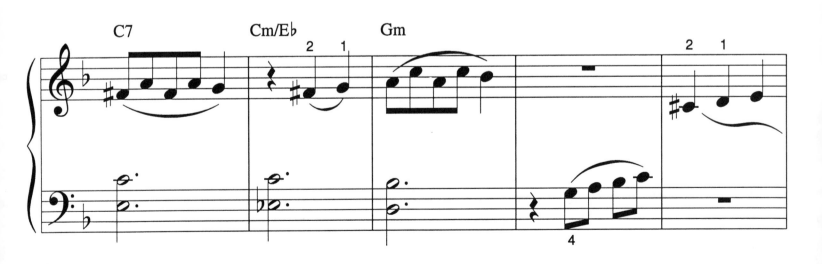